DESIGNING A SYSTEM THAT WORKS

ORGANIZATIONAL CHANGE AND A STUDY OF SYSTEMS

THE X SYSTEM

MARY NESTLE-HALLGREN

ISBN: 978-0-9655376-3-6

Author's note

In 1995 I presented the models described in this book at a seminar for the Justice Department in Denver Colorado. In those days I called it the positive vs. the negative model and since that time my view of it has gone through many revisions. At first there appeared to be two different opposing systems in the world but over time it became clear that the pervasive obvious overriding worldly system is what could be termed a dark X System of limitations with all its variations.

Another system not so physical but also available to all of us, is operating somewhat elusively and our awareness of it is constantly evolving. This is a system of possibilities, love, and light. We can use many words to name it. It envelopes the world available for us to tap into through our thoughts affecting behaviour and any system we participate in. It is through our thoughts that we create change in our world.

Our individual thinking causes us to constantly vacillate back and forth in our emotions between darkness and light as we learn from experience. At our basic level we are animals of survival and it is a luxury not to have to kill to eat. We are physical beings limited by our physical world. As we learn and become more enlightened it is comforting to know that we can improve relationships and build a system that works for improved outcomes even within the shadow of the physical world.

The goal of organizational change is looking for some improvement within a system within the world. We are all given vision which is light. Vision is looking for the possibility of more success or some higher outcome for an organization to reach that its entire people could see and move towards. Abundance and love is what the light system is all about. It takes tapping into the light through individual thinking to follow any vision. Vision has to be more than a selfish vision for it to have a gravitational pull towards light.

This same X system dynamic operates through any group be it families or a large organization. And, although it begins and ends with individual thoughts, we need a vision of that ultimate goal of what a system could become of total light, should we all wish to participate, in creation of systems based on something called love.

Although I start with a description of the worst of how our physical system operates, I give a counter example – a vision of the best of possible worlds to move towards. We participate on a daily basis, each moment and each inter-action through time, moving towards or away from either potential outcome of either system.

CONTENTS

PREFACE:
ORGANIZATIONS
AS SYSTEMS

This book is about the study of organizational systems and culture. Although culture is often defined as how things are done, I see it more as a *flavour* of the group. Culture is what we experience through our senses. Culture is the taste, smell, feeling, or resulting overriding attitude or mood of the whole group as they interact.

Using the metaphor of cooking, the smell of cooking lets you know something is being cooked even if you didn't know what was put in the pot. Our senses let us know which culture is brewing. Simply put, working in a system, the culture can be experienced as positive and happy or negative and unhappy. Working in some organizations actually **stinks**. Stinking thinking contributes to an overriding negative attitude of any group.

In this book I present two extremely different designs or models organizations might use and the underlying thinking that makes them one way or the other. Often named authoritarian or autocratic, this organizational type is experienced as negative, while one that is more synergistic will be experienced as positive. Whichever model is operating will determine the culture felt by the people in the group. In actuality, organizations operate as a continuum between these two models but it is useful to differentiate them by first seeing them separately. Through a closer examination you can decide as a leader which pieces are creating problems or what would make an improvement. The description in this book could be applied to a family system, any small group of two, or any large organization.

Thinking that creates a system includes concentration of power, expectations, how people interact, patterns of behaviour, meaning, philosophy, values, beliefs, and attitudes, as well as written and implied rules. How leadership and its people think and believe will determine the type of organizational structure, model, or system. It will be the whole structure with all the interrelating parts that define the model. The assumption is that a business is a living organism and follows some natural laws that cause it to evolve.

PREMISE

An organization has similarities to how a chemical compound is formed and how it bonds to become whole.

In science, wholeness theory is that nature is made up of separate independent elements that come together to create wholeness threw the process of organization, integration, and cooperation. I contend that nature intends, and that it is natural, for an organization to move toward wholeness. At least there is an intention to move in that direction. Vision is light. The vision of an organization is always a direction towards light or the wish for some improvement which is something positive. If there isn't progression towards wholeness, it is because there is some obstacle or negativity in thinking within the system.

Attraction gives elements a gravitational pull towards wholeness. When there are parts missing, mismatched, blocked, or left over, wholeness is impossible. Parts may be present but not integrated or only temporarily playing a part. Elements that don't fit promote imbalance. Imbalance in any system interferes but may still perform some function.

A whole compound can be broken into parts so in this study of systems, we want to first identify the model and then understand the parts and how, or if, they fit together for wholeness.

Elements combine to create some mixture or compound. Compounds are divided into two categories – Ionic and covalent.

Metals react with non-metals to form ionic compounds. Ionic compounds are composed of positive and negative ions **by adding or subtracting** electrons from neutral atoms or molecules. In other words, joining ionic compounds does not result in permanent wholeness. It is based on fragmentation, parts, and needs. The whole molecule is not used which contributes to waste. Only part is used which fills a temporary need.

Covalent compounds are composed of neutral molecules. Neutral molecules are whole and used as whole. Covalent bonding is when one or more pairs of electrons are **shared** by two atoms. Co means shared. People who are whole can work together without issues.

Ionic is to authoritarian as covalent is to synergistic. Applying the scientific idea to how people are organized and fit together gives us a different view of an organization as a compound. Stability of any system relates to the concept of wholeness.

We start by identifying the organization and then break it down into individual elements to understand how parts contribute to the whole operation. If the desired outcome was wholeness, that wholeness should be spread throughout the whole system and every part. The state of a system is determined by the level of organization, integration, and cooperation within its parts

The attempt at wholeness is lost if the underlying idea of the system is fragmentation. If the organization is held together through force, threat or some dysfunction, there would be imbalance and instability.

From a practical standpoint and a larger view, every business is trying to create wholeness in the world in some way by filling a need. When a business fills a need in the world, it becomes a viable business. If there were no needs to fill, we wouldn't have a reason for business. The discussion here is to examine wholeness from an organizational design perspective.

ORGANIZATIONAL ELEMENTS

Breaking an organization down to its elemental parts and how these parts operate together presents a unique picture. The elements are interactions between management and employees and how this occurs in relationships including the tiniest element - individual thought and emotion. What are the underlying ideas that hold this combination of elements together?

If there is a problem in organizations, it is because some idea or thought can't promote cooperation or integration which would be required for everyone to work together smoothly. Different elements fit together and form a compound that is whole where as others would be repelled or only temporarily fit in a mix.

How smooth an operation exists has to do with the willingness of cooperation and attraction for some mutually beneficial outcome. Any deficiency interferes with cooperation and integration. If each person is feeling whole and valued, the organization will run simply and easily.

In this study of organizations we are comparing two models. Some organizations operate in continuous instability while others pull together through cooperation and attraction. We will examine each element in the organization from individual thinking to leadership. The smallest element of any organization is the thinking of each individual and how that thinking fits with the whole larger mind of the organization.

HOW AN
ORGANIZATION THINKS
IS A FEEDBACK LOOP

Obviously all individuals including management behave as a result of the way they think. An idea is a thought. Thinking exits in feelings or emotions. Feelings drive behaviour. Behaviour, beliefs, and values are results of thinking that work together which create a system within a system. How people in the system think and what they believe affects the operation of the whole organization.

The way the whole system operates in return reverberates back to affect thinking and emotions, behaviour, beliefs, and values of its people. Although this feedback loop mostly begins and ends with leadership, the evaluation of systems here relates to thinking on all levels or the mind-set of everyone in the system.

We have two opposing styles of organizational models or systems – Authoritarian or Synergistic with a mix in between. This book compares these two systems as extremes and the elements that make them one system or another and how or why you would use one over the other.

We will start with the most common and disliked system used in organizations and government (authoritarian) following with the most idealized example of a synergistic model.

What is
Authoritarianism
vs. Synergism?

"Authoritarianism: A term political scientist's
use for a worldview that values order authority
and distrusts outsiders & social change."

https://www. youtube. com/watch?v=5YU9djt_CQM

It's a way of governing through rules and control and
imbalance of power similar to a dictator. Practice of
management in which orders are issued with threats
of punishment for disobedience, and which is based
on the belief that status and power differences in an
organization are appropriate and must be maintained.

http://www.businessdictionary.com/definition/authoritarianism.
html#ixzz49WhxUxfc.

Other definitions: favoring complete obedience
or subjection to authority as opposed to individual
freedom. Subordinate to the power or authority of the
state...exercising complete or almost complete control
over the will of another or others...Relating to blind

submission to authority. Expecting or requiring people to obey rules or laws: not allowing personal freedom.

http://www. merriam-webster. com/dictionary/authoritarian

Authoritarianism is usually some expectation of blind submission from a concentration of power, often carried out by an elite group. All of the above are describing the X System.

Synergism: combined action or operation, a mutually advantageous conjunction or compatibility of distinct business participants or elements (as resources or efforts)

https://www.merriam-webster.com/dictionary/synergy

WHAT IS A MODEL AND A SYSTEM?

*A **model*** *is a simplified version of a concept, phenomenon, relationship, system in the real world to explain and predict events on the basis of past observations containing only those feature that are of primary importance.*

*A **system*** *is a set of connected parts forming a complex whole working together as a mechanism in an interconnected network.*

The X System/ Model

The X System/Model is a description of the most extreme dark or negative and dysfunctional model of organization. This model is based on limitations. Each person within the system is somehow limited and in some way would cause conflict or feels conflicted. People can be together and stay within the system through control, force, or some dysfunction.

This system has a specific mind-set so discussions about behaviour and systems will be expressed from that point of view. Keep in mind that the X system is all about the Ego perception which is an uneducated limited view of the self in the world.

Here are 30 points that identify the X system followed by 30 improved ways to think or participate in any system. See if you recognize any of the following parts or ideas in your present world:

1. **It's a Hierarchy.** As an extreme this is a rigid hierarchy but it can be implied. Your value is your place in the hierarchy. You must keep this place and "not rock the boat."

   People are picked for a limited piece of the total operation and are supposed to stay within the boundaries of their small place. People are assumed to be of limited importance so only people that accept these limitations can fit. When limitation is a requirement, it makes dysfunction a requirement. Therefore, people are less than or more than others based on the hierarchy in place.

The only way to move up is if you can be superior. It has to be a perceived superiority that fits that particular system. If you are better looking or have more clout in some way there is leverage. It is always a power play to move up the ladder of importance. You must understand what holds a special hierarchy in place. If the system values degrees and you attain a special degree you can move up. What a system values is where the power is. If the system values how you look, you can move up based on that.

People are viewed as superior or inferior, more than or less than in every hierarchy based on its unique values. You have to understand the specialness within each hierarchy, not on what is said, but on what you observe, to be valued. All power comes from how high up you in perceived importance. Nothing is mutual or equal. The hierarchy is held together by outside force and is always at risk of an upset. Strict boundaries keep it held in place.

People lower in the hierarchy are told what to do, how to think, and how to be. People are working against each other because they are in competition for importance or at least think they are. Space or place must be clearly defined so that the place will fit the right people. Knowing your place or the boundary imposed is key to not overstepping where you belong.

2. **Identity.** One's identity is tied to one's place in the hierarchy so the mind-set of the individuals in this group is focused on the exterior of what others think. It's all about show so that is why people brag about themselves. The roles you play, your title, your position in the hierarchy, your degree, what you have or do is who you are. No one can be authentically who they really are because their place in the hierarchy of importance defines them. Because of this, confidence is a façade. "Fake it till you make it."

Everyone is pretending they are something they are not. Egos are always concerned about what other people think of them because the place you occupy is set by others. Saving face is the only thing that counts. Who others think you are is who you are.

It's a rat race to acquire. The more you have the better off you think you are. Winning and acquiring stuff is what it is about and helps to define you. If you have stuff, you must be somebody. If you don't have stuff you are nobody. If you have more than others, a bigger house, a more expensive car, the more others think you are, the more important you can pretend to be.

The underlying thinking of what you have or do, or what others think you have, is what you are. What you are is only in relationship to what others don't have. How people view you is who you are so it is very important to impress. Everything is measured by what others think. Save the best for company because what others think is more important than the truth. People get crushed by what others think of them.

3. **Rules**. Many rules are the first sign you have an X System operating. Rules define place and importance so must be rigidly enforced. Don't think, follow the rules. It is all about obeying the rules even if the rules seem stupid or make little sense. Often the rules are not clear and can change by the hierarchy at any moment, so you can't do anything right. Just when you think you've got it all figured out, someone pulls the rug out from under you.

Often there is a need to report or call others out if we see them not obeying the rules. This is a normal tendency as we are all so programmed to find fault with others. Follow the leader, and try to raise yourself up by getting someone else in trouble. We often hold others to standards we don't hold for ourselves. What is the difference between rules and principles? Principles require thinking to follow them.

Protocol is a company's official procedures or system of rules governing behaviors. Pre-decision is useful for systems that are at risk if people start to think for themselves. It is a way of keeping people in line. The hierarchy is dependent on each person keeping their place.

Any time you are walking on eggs you are in the X System. It is about thinking. We can generalize this thinking to one person or to a family, organization, or larger government system. Not following the rules makes you "wrong" in this system even if you thought you were doing something kind and loving.

Rules don't apply to you if you are the authority (the one making the rules) or have enough money, position, and or power to overrule. Punishment is quickly used to enforce rules and exercise control. So beware.

Loyalty is to the system and rules, not to personal principles, so people don't own themselves. Rules in an X System are often insinuated but not spoken. "Be seen and not heard" and, "Don't question authority." In general, don't question anything. Don't tell. There is an assumption you will keep secrets. Any rule that is not in the highest good of everyone or any systems that make rules that don't work so they have to make another rule for the exception is X system. Rules are made to control, to keep the hierarchy in place, and are made for the lowest common denominator in this system.

There are rules of the road so everyone can be safe. Rules are not all bad as some hold functions. In large systems, functional rules are so everyone can work together better. Rules should be guidelines, not rigid road blocks. However, the less rigid a system is, the more functional the participants need to be.

4.   **Mistakes are a big deal.** Making a mistake in a rigid system is wrong. It is like a sin. Getting caught is terrifying. If making a mistake is too big of a deal, you won't be able to trust that people will tell the truth. There will always be a cover-up.

People resist change if problems are a big deal. If change means there was a problem, there will be resistance and fear. When people are stuck there is fear going on, they don't like change. They know how to deal with the present problems and don't want to risk something even worse that is unknown. People operating in this system assume that if you have to change something, something was wrong.

You can't admit that you need to learn because that makes you less than someone else as knowledge is power. Not knowing might cause you to be lowered in the system.

Everything is either right or wrong. There is no grey area in a system of rules. To be made wrong is almost annihilation. It is important not to question what is believed to be right in the system. Do as you are told.

As a leader, what is a "right" according to you needs to be clearly defined for others. If you find that people are not doing what you think is right, take responsibility. Perhaps they didn't know how to read your mind or maybe it was just a mistake that could be forgiven. Did they agree to the limitations you expected them to abide by? Was there clear communication about the limitations? Did people feel free to leave the system if they didn't want those limitations? Can they leave or must they fight back or rebel?

The problem in government is that people have limited freedom to leave the system. We are somewhat stuck in our country of origin. It is a hierarchy that we have limited influence over leadership. It is a system of rules. We have varying degrees of limitations as people and so the rules needed are made to cover all possible limitations.

5. **Drama.** Highlight drama. Anytime you see it, hear it, or feel it, you are experiencing an

X System event. Drama happens anytime a person expresses something negative. Anytime a person tells their story with too many details, it is drama.

Any negative feeling expressed or defensive reaction will create drama. Limiting communication limits drama. This is why in many places people don't talk to each other. If there is too much communication, you might trigger some hidden emotion that will come back on you. Communication opens up opportunity to vent.

Drama is normal when people feel limited, needy, or powerless. Drama is a way to shift the uneven distribution of power in a hierarchy.

Drama becomes a habit. People often crave drama as an outlet. Some people can't live without it. Life would be too boring and they have nothing good to share.

6. **Negative.** This is a negative system so the focus is on looking for what's wrong. People live in negativity feeling worthless, helpless, and hopeless and depressed or numb. This system is stressful. People are trying to figure out how to survive the system so everyone is on edge and not happy.

Although it is discouraged to show negativity, people are being hurt all the time. They don't feel considered or respected.

Sometimes only a Pollyanna approach is allowed so people fake being positive or nice. Since most people are living in negative emotions, it is natural to be reactive and be fake. You have to be ready to defend every action. Everyone takes what is said to them from their own personal limited view so everything is taken personally. Don't take it personally. It is just business in the X system.

Some people become immune to emotions or supress their emotions until they shut down. Then behaviour becomes automatic and robotic.

Since emotions drive behaviour, a business would do best to only hire people that can manage their emotions if they want creativity. Creativity is blocked by bad feelings. One of the problems of today is that the younger generation has more difficulty working in an X system organization. (See "The Emotion Revolution" at the end of this book as to why) Also read "Help for the Victim Entitlement Epidemic" recently published. Many new organizations built by young people are more synergistic than in the past. The world is changing very fast.

7. **Bonding.** Bonding in this system is through some deficit. This can be done by taking sides and sometimes on being against the company or other people they work with. Negative people bond on misery and their issues. People

who share similar problems or addictions use these dysfunctions to connect. They bond on what's wrong or what they can complain about in life.

No one is whole so people bond by getting one's needs met or filling needs. If everyone feels insecure or dependent, the whole system bonds on dysfunction as people are completing or seeking to be completed.

Bonding negatively becomes a habit. Bonding when feeling bad is trying to fill yourself up through someone else because you can't find enough of yourself to feel whole alone.

If there is no way to get away from a negative system, bonding on the negative is the only option. Most people who work in an X system environment need a happy home to leave work for so they have some balance to recover.

8. **Don't question.** Authority is always right in a rigid X system. "Do as I say, not as I do." Authority doesn't have to follow the same rules its subjects have to follow. Questioning authority is disrespectful because one would be challenging truth. It is not about truth. You can't question rules, how things are done, or authority. Issues here are not open to discussion for good reason - they can't be explained.

Individuals who grew up in an X system family already know these rules and know how to work around them. They do as they please behind your back, manipulate, pretend to be good, take liberties where possible, and are never direct.

9. **Win/lose or lose/win.** Position, power, or winning over, is one of the identifying marks of the X System. Individuals set themselves and others up to win/lose, lose/win, or no/win. If you aren't a winner, you are a loser. It is not about the journey or being in the moment, it is about getting to the end goal. Anyone a winner is only temporarily on top. No matter what you do you can't really win. In a closed system, every win creates a loss. Someone is always losing because of the limited supply.

   This system is all about winning because of the pervasive idea that there is only so much to go around. It is the idea or belief of limitation that makes it closed. It is like the whole world is in some kind of bubble or balloon and the only air available is what is in the balloon. Every breath is limiting air for others.

   There is only so much business in the world. There are only so many people to sell to. Whatever you believe is true for you. Focusing on limitation creates the idea that you are in competition everywhere. If there is limited supply, then your gain must be someone else's loss. Pop the balloon. Believe that whatever business you need is there for you and you can change your perception. Beliefs are just opinions and perceptions held in this limited X System.

10. **Survival, Scarcity, and Sacrifice.** People have to survive this system. There is so much scarcity. It is a constant battle. There is never enough. You can never be enough or do enough. There is never enough to go around. There is not room at the top for more. Lack and limitation is everywhere.

Sacrifice is honoured or expected because of the overall limitations. Companies expect you to sacrifice and do overtime or put them before family or other things in life. In this system, sacrifice and martyrdom are often a way to be valued.

The company is trying to pay employees as little as possible and take from customers as much as possible. Employees are doing as little as possible. Everyone is living in scarcity. Everyone is cheap or looking for free. That is why there is such a race to the bottom on price.

Because the competition is so tough, the system is abusive to people emotionally and they have to be in survival mode. Thinking survival creates even more survival behaviour and becomes a vicious cycle.

11. **Pretending.** Everyone is pretending to be happy. Everyone pretends they are OK; things are OK, and pretending they are something they are not.

People abide by office politics pretending they agree on everything and that is one way to get along. Pretend you like the same things. Pretend you believe the same as others. It's a pretend life.

People pretend they are friends but you have to watch what they say behind your back.

It is said, "Once they stop talking to you, they start talking about you."

Companies pretend they are making money and adjust the books. If they are beholding to stockholders, it is a great temptation to cook the books. They don't own themselves any more than employees own themselves working in the same kind of system.

12. **Integrity.** Authority says, "Do as I say, not as I do." There is no real integrity. People tell you what you want to hear to keep peace or to stop you from reacting. It isn't about truth. People rarely know how they feel about anything. A person's moral compass is outside them. The end justifies the means.

Scamming people is easy because they are not in touch with their inner knowing - they are in touch with their addictions, limiting beliefs, games they are playing, and pretending. There is no honesty here so don't expect it. People do what they can get away with. This is only a problem if you get caught and authority is always trying to catch you.

13. **Competition.** This system is constant serious competition. It is life and death competition because competition is tied to identity and importance which is everything that has value in this system. Since everyone is in competition, no one is really safe or can be trusted. Compete to get ahead. Measurement is compared to someone else or what should be.

Competition pits people against each other. Business competition is a dog eat dog world. Thinking creates a competitive market fighting for a small piece of the pie.

14. **Control**. Most people are either controlling others or feeling out of control. It is a system of control. Control is so important mainly because of how rules are looked at. If you are not sure about the rules, you would be constantly in fear of violation and consequences. Constantly wondering and not knowing takes people off balance which makes them feel out of control.

People have to control outside because they feel out of control inside. Anytime you feel the need for boundaries someone is trying to control you or has overstepped. Controlling what people think is a high priority –reality doesn't matter.

It is a high priority of X management to have everything controlled. If you have to answer to higher management why something has happened that could be seen as a negative, you might share in some consequences. If you are upper management and have no connection with lower management, you would need to have many rules designed to let people know how they are supposed to act because you are out of touch. Any person violating a rule is a power shift and must be dealt with.

15. **Communication.** Communication is limited, minimal, withheld, absent, antagonistic, argumentative, combative, secretive, controlling or controlled, automatic, robotic, and reactive. The system is not set up for truth so communication needs to be limited so secret information won't slip out.

You will be judged by what you say and what you reveal can be used against you. You are never safe. Words are open to interpretation and everyone has their own meaning. People are always talking behind other people's back to raise themselves up. One has to be very careful about what others know.

One company tried a new approach. The intention was to open up conversation to improve the company culture. In one meeting the hired coach asked everyone to unload all the things they never got to say. He thought that if people would get stuff off their chests, the culture would improve. That just got people in trouble. If you don't change the thinking behind a problem, changing behaviour won't work.

Everyone has their beliefs they are locked into. Arguments are common when opinions are beliefs. Combative communication is about the struggle for power in this system. It is all about being right. Everyone has to be "right" to be OK so sharing becomes arguing rather than discussion. You would have to make it safe for people to tell the truth.

16. **Secrets.** Since no one is safe or OK in this system we have to keep secrets about everything so we won't be judged. Secrets are used to show loyalty and take sides. Secrets protect our safety while we share those secrets about someone else to create specialness. Also, "knowledge is power" so if you keep your mouth shut, others can assume you know more than you do. How you are seen by others is so important that

no one can really disclose the truth about themselves.

17. **Distrust.** This system distrusts employees and employees distrust management. Management has to put up surveillance cameras to watch people. This is understandable as people are human and make mistakes. So even in Synergistic companies it is important to keep one's eyes open.

When people see or suspect corruption in management they lose respect. They naturally already distrust management since the same rules don't apply to them. When employees are paid as little as possible and feel taken advantage of, they make up for lack of pay by stealing or taking advantage any way they can. It's a quiet war.

18. **Information.** Information is used to control and for power and position. Privy to information gives you importance. Finding something out about someone, that they don't want others to know, can be used as leverage.

Some information is on a need to know basis and protected even in more Synergistic organizations. But it is the mind-set and practicality behind the action that makes the difference.

19. **Position, Prestige, and Money** is most important. This is a hierarchy of values. These are end goals in this system in place of happiness. This system is not about happiness, it is about survival. Position is a means to get money. Prestige is a means to influence for power and money.

The mind-set is, if you can just get ahead, or ever have enough, you will then be happy. If you can move up, it means happiness. It is always about getting somewhere else.

If you have enough money, you may be able to buy your way out of most any situation as money means power here.

20. **Passive or aggressive.** These are roles that are played. There is room for only one aggressive person in any situation or it would be war. Everyone else has to step to passive. Passive people don't challenge others so they get along better and don't rock the boat. Passive people absorb the pressure. Aggressive people always win because they have the most skills but if you can't win, go passive and blame. Aggressive people bully others to control and win over.

21. **Manipulation.** People have to manipulate to get what they want while pretending they don't want. Nothing is direct or upfront in an X system. You can't directly ask, so people learn to

manipulate and use leverage. Somehow, you are never allowed be direct. You can't say you took the day off for the real reason; it has to be some bonafide excuse. This is often because someone has to answer to someone else higher up.

Manipulating is a way of getting what you want without really asking. The goal is to get someone to offer what you want by talking about some need and getting another person to agree that the need should be filled. That might trick them into offering help to meet that goal. If you have to ask for something, it means you are lower or lesser than someone else, so it is difficult to ask.

Complaining is an indirect way of asking for something. You are hoping someone will agree with you that something is wrong and as a result, something will change but you want someone else to take the action. Complaining is somewhat acceptable as a way of voicing in the X system. Negativity is tiresome and drama. Pressuring others to act for you and using influence are other ways to manipulate.

22. **Destructive & Dysfunctional**. Destroy others so you can win. If you make a mistake, destroy all evidence you even tried. Any destructive behaviour is X. Or maybe, an X system causes destructive behaviour. Operating in the X system turns happiness into self-

gratification. Most people here are both dysfunctional and in some way destructive. The System is destructive to a person's wellbeing while at the same time the system is dealing with people who are dysfunctional. Many times this is because the organization is too cheap to hire qualified people and more qualified people would challenge the system.

23. **Selfish or selfless.** Selfish is considered bad but selfish people are the ones who usually get what they want. It's all about "Me" from both perspectives as both are seeing any situation from their small limited point of view. People who can't win over find a different kind of win by being selfless. Selflessness is sometimes honoured and often rewarded. If everyone was selfless the organization would be at an advantage.

This system is made up of extremes as people are either more or less in the hierarchy. People are givers or takers and flip between selfish and selfless. Some value in limitation could be found either way.

24. **Must document everything.** You are always at risk of being written up. Document everything to keep yourself safe. This is especially true when dealing with anything government. Authority documents all your mistakes just to

get rid of you or have power over you. You must document, document, document to stay out of trouble or defend yourself in this authoritative system.

Although it is always good to document, in the X system there is a great need to be on the defensive as it is so much about blame. You often have to prove or support that you were abiding by the rules.

25. **Motivation**. Motivation is threat based and creates high stress. If you don't do what's right, punishment will happen. People live in fear of their jobs being threatened. If you do perform well, management might expect even more at a later time, so people do as little as possible. Often performance is measured according to some unknown standard because in this system, nothing is made clear. Clarity works against this system. It is about keeping people off balance.

Any fear is motivating: fear of failure, fear of not measuring up, fear of not being liked. If people are working because of economic pressure, emotional pressure, or even inertia, they won't perform at their best.

X system workplace is always high stress. External force to perform is levied through guilt, shame, fear, peer pressure, avoiding disappointment, avoiding punishment, or only to gain economic reward. All of these ways of motivating oneself or others hurts performance.

26. **Co-dependency.** Usually there is an extreme about people either being too dependent or overly independent. Overly independent people don't ask for help and try to do everything themselves, while micromanaging others. These people think they are the only capable people.

People who don't know they have value complete others to feel worthwhile or lean on others to be OK. People end up overly dependent on the system or others, needy and dependent, looking to get their needs filled outside them. People live in dependency fearful of losing others, favours, and importance.

Rescuing is part of co-dependency and dysfunctional. Rescuing someone so they don't experience their own consequences of their decisions is not helpful and keeps people from learning from life.

It is believed that how you make others feel is your fault as well as being responsible for others. These underlying beliefs are at the basis of all co-dependency. Organizations don't know better so they dysfunctionally support this and support victims. If you make someone else feel bad, they are a victim of you.

The truth is that you can't make anyone feel anything they choose not to feel. So you can't always be responsible for how other people feel as a response to you. Now this can be taken the wrong way. If you are mean, you are responsible for your own meanness and what it creates for you. It will come back on you. For every stimulus there is a response.

Caretaking is pretended caring or dysfunctional caring. Evidence is all around us of pretended caring. The writing on the plastic bag of toilet paper says "to avoid suffocation...." But, it really is about looking good to the public and protection.

27. **Head Games** played – blaming, victim, entitlement, punishment, silent treatment, exclusion, criticism, condemnation, complaints, obligation, guilt, and pity. Games are always played to get power or shift value in an indirect way. The blame game is played to shift attention and point fingers if someone is caught. Victim attitude is another way to blame or shift responsibility. Victims have power in this system if they can get support behind their victimhood. The danger is that victims make other people victims. Entitlement is the new problem. Punishment can be dealt through silent treatment or exclusion. Criticism or condemning others is a way to put others down. Complaining is a way to get what you want by making someone else look like the problem.

Obligation and guilt is a way to motivate others to get what you want if they will buy into that. Pity is either a way to make someone less than you or to get someone to come your way by them feeling sorry for you. It may be a way to get attention or get someone to side with you. Winning at games can have either an emotional or monetary reward.

There are two options when someone is playing games with you. You can either ignore them or call them on their game. People can't play these games if you don't care or if you don't have anything invested in their game. Stop participating. It's about winning over. If there is no communication, they can't win anything. All these games are dysfunctional behaviours.

28. **Rebel, revolt, and retaliate**. If people get fed up they rebel, revolt and sometimes retaliate. These are behaviours of negative aggressiveness against the X System. Management can only push people so far before they push back. Give them any hope, then take it away, and rebellion is insured.

People who have a victim mentality will almost always retaliate because they want to inflict pain to make up for their loss. If they feel they are wronged, they want to push the point of what they feel is right. It is more about the principle to them, that they were victimized and so now they need to make you a victim to get even.

29. **Boundaries.** In the X system, boundaries are a problem because rules are not clear. If people don't know where the boundaries are, they don't know where to stand in line. It is common for people to overstep boundaries or have none because the boundaries are relative to the system not a person's internal integrity. Boundaries for organizations need to be clearly outlined and documented, not assumed.

The rules are boundaries set up to limit freedoms. If you are having too much fun, you must not be working. Work is not supposed to be about fun in this system. Work is work. Happiness doesn't compute.

Don't get too close to people in an X system. Familiarity breeds contempt. The problem is that people are protective because they don't want you to know too much about them so they put up boundaries to keep a distance. People already judge themselves so if you are close enough to see their faults they will be afraid of being judged. You might find yourself at risk of some fallout or trigger their emotions. When you get close and boundaries are lost you become like family and family doesn't get the best in this system. The best is saved for company and that also includes manners.

Accomplishing, needs filled, or winning over are the main means to happiness here. Getting needs filled is another way to feel happiness. Getting attention, winning some reward, getting something over someone else, are ways people feel good. Don't take any freedoms for granted. Rules dictate the amount of freedom available. People don't expect to be free or they wouldn't be here.

30. **Respect**. Respect has to do with who you are according to the system rather than being respected for who you really are. Respect is given for position, age, importance, or power not because it is earned. People can't respect themselves because they don't measure up to some outside standard that is never clear. People don't respect themselves because they can't have integrity in this system. Respect is often shown just to inflate someone else's ego.

RESULTS OF
THE X SYSTEM

This system keeps people in their place and is autocratic or authoritarian. However, working in an X system is pressure and stressful affecting health. This system will not work where creativity or good customer service is important. People will work only because they have to for financial reasons.

Often employees sabotage the company by doing little things to get even. They will be trying to make up for what they feel entitled to have. No one feels safe. Most people feel negative. Production and performance will suffer. Product quality and safety may suffer. Respect for leadership will suffer.

This system is useful during crisis if there isn't time to think and one must follow the leader but, that would be a temporary situation. A form of the X system is used in the military where it is clearly defined.

As a leader, what you do is more important than what you say. Many companies tell you the organization is like a family but it turns out that it is a big dysfunctional family. Employees know if you can walk your talk or if the rules only apply to them. They will not respect you or the system if this is the case. It is clear that dysfunctional limited people held together by outside means will create temporary outcomes and invite chaos unless there is constant control. This is not about happiness – it is about survival.

If you want good customer service you won't get that from unhappy employees. If employees are part of a happy team they will naturally treat your customers better.

DO YOU NEED TO CHANGE THE ORGANIZATIONAL STRUCTURE?

That depends on the outcome you want. It also depends on the capabilities and thinking of leadership as well as the thinking of employees. If customer satisfaction is not an issue and you just want to keep people in line, the X system may work for you at least on a limited or temporary basis. There can be a form of functional X system as long as the system is clearly stated and agreed upon. All systems are a mix between both systems, so be sure you have written expectations to fall back on.

Notice which X system issues are going on in your family or organization. How are you contributing to the way the system is operating in your own thinking and behaviours?

High customer satisfaction is linked to strong happy workplace cultures. Workers today consider the culture of any company as important as salary and benefits. Employee retention is high when the culture is good.

To some degree, an organization's culture is always changing. The way it operates is the sum total of all the people within it. As ideas and people change, business practices and culture change in response.

How do you Change Culture?

Culture change won't work unless the thinking of the individual employees thinking changes along with management. People who think like X will only fit in an X system. Business is not usually considered to be the place for emotional change but know that thinking drives feelings and behaviour, so you can affect thinking.

The skills of confidence, self-worth, tact, patience are all emotional skills. If I work with an individual's emotional skills without working with management in an X organization, they will eventually leave that organization once they have developed enough skills. They will develop the courage to leave you. They will choose happiness over money and have the faith and trust that they can replace you. They will risk anything for freedom.

Hire only people who fit the system of the company you already have or that matches your leadership style. Change leadership first. Culture changes because the thinking in the system has changed. Once a leader has enough skills to handle an improved system, he or she can slowly institute changes and grow the people to fit a new desired system or replace with people that fit the system they prefer.

Different ways of thinking create very different results. Each model is a way of thinking and acting that works together as a system that produces some results. Would changing the system produce the results you are looking for?

The ideas or beliefs a person lives by operate together and fit into one overriding system or the other. A way of thinking and being, in a system, contributes to the larger system. Each individual in any organization is part of the total of how that system operates. Changing any part affects the whole. Adding one new person can change the whole system. Each entity in that organizational system is part of the whole entity – the organization.

There has to be a transition of improved thinking to move into a new system. As an employee, thinking a new way can upset you or the system. Begin by changing your ideas about making mistakes. See them as opportunities to learn so you don't take on guilt and shame. Develop your tact, confidence, and self-esteem. Learn to know who you are when you are whole outside the system and then bring that wholeness into the system.

If you are the owner you can give people opportunities to develop new emotional skills by helping them think differently. Do this, not by inflating their ego, but by educating, inspiring, and encouraging. Use the following model of ideas and concepts to gradually change thinking and a system.

THE SYNERGISTIC ORGANIZATIONAL MODEL

1. **Equality.** This model values performance over seniority. It collaborative and is about working together for a common goal which is automatically more team oriented. If you are the leader, you will need to define this common goal and get people behind it.

In this system, people are considered equal which is why it is not a hierarchy. Hierarchy is a mind-set. If you don't see others as an equal, they will know it. People who don't feel equal will show it. Understand what creates real equality in people's minds. It is about creating a mind-set that believes that life is a unique learning journey and everyone is perfect where they are on their journey and everyone is making a unique contribution.

Accepting that every person has a unique individual journey is accepting that everyone has an individual reason for being here. None of us have the same opportunity, gifts, beginnings or experience and need to accept this difference without judgment. We are all different and no one fits the same box. We are perfect in our individual uniqueness. The only thing that makes us equal is that we all have a unique life journey and make a unique contribution. In no other way are we equal.

Where ever you are on your journey is perfect for you. You are already perfect you don't have to try to be something you are not. You may not have felt like you were the perfect parent or the perfect child but, you were perfect for the experience the other person got. The problem is that we also have to accept that we give other people lessons in life that we didn't intend. There are always unintended consequences that we didn't expect. Have faith that others can forgive, have the willingness to learn, and can take responsibility for their own learning journey. We are all perfect on our journey in an imperfect world. The world is imperfect so that we have an opportunity to learn.

Everyone works together recognizing differences along with contributions. In this system, all opinions are considered valid. People are paid in line with their contribution and valued for their contribution as well as being valued as a person.

2. **Identity.** If people really know who they are they can set aside their ego and be real. It takes acceptance of self, one's journey whatever that is, and acceptance of others to be authentic. Who you are in reality is not a measurement of money,

position, or power. Take it all away and you are still uniquely you without any outside trappings.

This system allows a person to be authentic and real because it is safe. Recognize authentic informal leaders who are powerful allies in this organization. They are great influencers with others to be and do their best. They will drive an improved culture.

Everyone has an ego because they have a body. But healthy egos don't push other people around, and can be set aside making it possible to learn from experience. Set aside your ego as a leader and be real. You will always be learning from the journey of life. Our Egos need to learn to be whole.

What you think of you is more important than what others think. What others think of you will affect you but it needs to be in a balance. Sometimes it is important to dress the part but the emphasis is more how you feel about yourself and recognizing you are just playing a role.

How you take care of yourself tells others how you feel about yourself. Self-care is important. You do it for you because you value yourself.

3. **Rules.** Make it a rule to do what works for the highest good of all, rather than just follow rules. Think about what makes sense. Rules are contextual and don't always work. Use principles to guide actions. Some rules as guidelines are made so everyone can be on the same page. In this system,

if there is some flexibility and safety, rules can be questioned and revamped if they don't work.

4. **Mistakes = Learning.** In the synergistic system, mistakes are just part of the process of learning. If you learn something, it is a success. There is no such thing as failure. People in this system don't believe in failure. You are more valuable after having learned from a mistake. There is always something to learn.

Management needs to be flexible enough to recognize that everyone has their own truth. Everyone comes into the world knowing nothing and gains skills as they grow and learn. Discussion from the point of looking for what works for all, helps people find the information they need to cooperate and integrate.

Most the time it isn't about right vs. wrong, it is about doing what works for the highest good of everyone. However, if you are dealing with a system that doesn't look at mistakes as learning, you may need the courage to explain yourself and admit a mistake in that system and be willing to take whatever consequence that comes with that. Life is a learning journey and mistakes are just something to learn from.

What I learned from one friend is, what would be called an Unforgivable mistake in one person's world can be completely different then what it would be in someone else's world. In my world no mistake is Unforgivable.

The universe will always respond if you make a mistake and then fix it not just on your side but also on their side. If it's not fixed for the other person, you have really completed all your learning. If you hadn't gotten all the learning out of it the universe may wait to respond. Have faith in that. Work on an issue until you have realized all the sides of it and healed all parts of it.

In some types of businesses, the possibility of a mistake could have dire consequences. If you are the leader of an organization, be sure people feel safe and know any consequences. You have to change your idea of mistakes before you can pass this idea on.

Not everything is either right or wrong. Often there are grey areas. Thinking people can discuss what works and have a moral compass to guide them. Start by catching employees doing something right. Look for what is good. Spread the idea that it is OK to be wrong by telling your employees what you have learned. Focus on the positive and what works. What you focus on expands.

5. **Peace.** When people feel valued and have good communication and connection with each other there will be peace not drama. People with kindness and consideration will support peace. People need to know how to talk about their lives in a positive way. They need to know how to bottom line problems to cut the drama. Too many details are overwhelming.

Peace and harmony are the goals here. People have to *want* to get along. They have to desire peace. Hire people who are kind and considerate and positive. Show your people consideration to get consideration.

6. **Positive.** This is a positive system with positive people. The focus is abundance and freedom. People feel positive and happy. It takes happy people to create a happy system. Happiness is a choice. You can't make people happy if they choose not to be happy. You have to hire people that are already happy people. People who feel good about where they are will have a good attitude. Attitude is everything. Attitude is a choice. One bad apple can spoil the whole lot. Get rid of people who don't support a positive culture.

Positive people that feel good about themselves can recognize when another person is not at their best and not take it personally. They can step back and observe. They stay objective during discussions. They know if they are pushing their opinions on others. The business environment needs people able to be objective and positive.

7. **Bonding.** People in this system bond on similar values, beliefs, and interests. People bond on projects and sharing. Bonding in a synergistic system is always on something positive.

Learning and Change are high values. Change often means progress. You have reached a new level. Growth minded people love learning and change. Look for people who like to learn when hiring. Identify people who are dysfunctional and bond on dysfunction to keep them out of your system. Pity me and other mind games people play doesn't fit here.

8. **Question everything**. If authority allows for questioning there is room for growth. Question everything and only truth will remain.

   As you learn to think for yourself and develop the skills to question authority, use tact and patience. Be sure you are in a positive state of mind when questioning anyone because they will pick up a judgmental attitude. If you are holding any negative thoughts, others can tell, and they will react in kind. Work on your own feelings before you tackle any issue that has the possibility of triggering a reaction from others.

   In a leadership position, you have to make it safe for people to question. Give them permission to offer ideas and question. Give reasons for why things are done a certain way.

9. **All/Win.** Sometimes it is a win/win but even better is an all/win. If anyone loses, it is not an all/win. Synergistic companies want to be fair with everyone. If you want lasting success, make it a win for everyone.

10. **Abundance.** Everyone is working for a community success and is helpful with others. If the attitude and goal is abundance and freedom for all, all will thrive. To create this kind of environment, you have to see the best in people, believe there is something good about everything, even if it means you have to learn something. Create a fun atmosphere. Make work fun.

As an individual, if you feel you are sacrificing, take another look. Maybe you need to ask for more or you should put your talents elsewhere. Sacrificing is not right. If what you did was a sacrifice, then what you did didn't work for the highest good of all. Sometimes you can only see this in hindsight. There is no need for sacrificing in a positive system.

It is healthy for everyone to take care of themselves first and others second. People who believe in sacrifice don't understand their value. This would throw the system into an imbalance. Don't allow people to sacrifice for you – pay them what they are worth.

Generosity should be done because it feels right or out of love without strings not because a person is seeking value. People who sacrifice or are martyrs feel owed and will be trouble.

All your needs and wants are met. What you have is not who you are. You always have what you need and having more than someone else doesn't make you better. It is OK to acquire but not as an end all. Having an abundant attitude creates more abundance. You can always choose more. As a leader you can be a good example because you have done well for yourself. Give your employees the opportunity to also do well for themselves. Share abundance and you will have even more abundance.

Abundance is everywhere. It's a mind-set. If everyone is coming from abundance and freedom, the organization will benefit tremendously and everyone will be happy. Abundance and freedom are attitudes that create more of the same.

Freedom is of the mind and means different things to different people. Some people need flexible hours to feel free. It is about choice. No choice takes away the feeling of freedom. Attitude is everything.

11. **Authentic.** Everyone is OK on their journey when the system is synergistic. No one has to pretend in this system. If people are really OK with themselves and their lives they can be real. They won't be hiding who they are. They won't need to pretend they are something they are not.

Give people permission to be who they are and support an atmosphere of acceptance. If you don't pretend to be something you are not, others will feel more comfortable to be whoever they are. Take yourself off your own pedestal. The more people feel they can live out loud, the healthier the system and the people in it.

12. **Integrity.** Integrity is to your word and is one of the closest things to who you really are. In a Synergistic system everyone is operating out of integrity. People know how to be on time and keep their word. Their moral compass is inside them guiding them. They operate from good moral principles because the system is set up so people can be honest and tell the truth.

13. **Competition.** Competition in a synergistic system is fun competition. Everyone is coming from wholeness so they don't feel challenged in a negative way by the system or others.

    Now as a leader, you can't make other people whole if they feel unhappy and limited. You can send them for help. You can support ideas that help people feel OK about themselves. If you have a bunch of people living in fear and insecurity they won't support wholeness. Bring in someone to support the development of skills. Put a system in place that allows for happiness and fun.

    Although this is a competitive world, you are not in competition when you believe the right business will come to you that is right for you. No one can take away what is yours.

14. **Self-Control and empowered.** No control is needed if everyone has the skills for self-control and feels empowered. All the elements that go with a

synergistic system are empowering for individuals. People need self-control not outside control.

If you have people with addictions and lack of patience they may need help with these issues. If you empower people that have a big ego, they will upset the system or miss use power. Only empower people who can handle themselves.

15. **Communication.** Communication needs to be abundant so that everyone can be on the same page. Everyone can live and let live so they feel free to say what is needed. There would be no reason to hold back. Good respectful communication is valued in this system.

Good communication requires tack and respect. Good communication is back and forth action not one sided. People have discussions and share ideas and concepts rather than beliefs they are locked into. Opinions are just opinions and people who prefer discussions won't argue.

In the middle of writing this book I had an experience that had to do with communication. I was in the middle of writing it and there was an extreme intensity that went with the deadline. Writing a book is more like telling someone something, and is not the same kind of communication that goes with coaching. Coaching is includes hearing the other person. One has to not just tell but listen.

I took a break from writing to have a session with a new person and had not mentally prepared myself or taken a long enough break from writing to change my headspace. I came off as talking too much, not waiting to hear what she was really asking for, and operating on an assumption of what I assumed she needed, not giving her a chance to let me know what she really needed. Connecting through coaching is connecting on that soul level which doesn't happen if one person is caught in their telling state.

There is a difference between results and experience. In this coaching situation she may have gotten some results but the experience she felt was different than what she expected or desired. I learned something as a result. There is a mutual reason for every connection. Every connection is some kind of opportunity. Every connection is for some mutual benefit and mutual learning.

16. **Open and honest.** There is a difference between keeping secrets rather than choosing not to disclose something. Not everyone is capable of hearing the truth or needs to hear everything. Everyone is entitled to a private life that needs to be respected. Not disclosing something personal is not a lie. If a system is open and invites honesty, people won't be afraid to tell the truth. Encourage courage and positive beliefs. In a synergistic system, the consequences are shared by all. People work together to solve problems.

17. **Trust.** A collaborative synergistic system will support trust. Without trust this system cannot stay in place. People need to feel safe and trusted. Backing each other up with mutual support and respect as well as good communication builds trust and makes for great culture.

Don't be stupid either. Blind trust is not part of the synergistic system. People are human and have issues. Trust is needed in many areas. You need to trust that people won't steal. You need to trust that people have integrity. Fairness promotes trust. Open up conversations to talk about this topic. Learn about your people so you know them well enough to trust them. Anyone that is pervasively negative or acts desperate is a risk.

To live in a positive system takes faith and trust not just in you but also others and something more than this. Any time this is lost, there is just something to learn. Learn what is needed and take back your faith and trust. Connect on a soul level with someone else that loves you and that you can reach on that level and you will find yourself.

18. **Information.** All information is shared that is needed. The intention is open communication and information. The more people know, the more they can contribute and collaborate.

19. **Happiness for all is the highest goal.** Money and acquiring are only two of the means to the end goal

of happiness. Money is important; it just isn't the end all. Prestige mostly feeds the ego and makes people jealous. Your value doesn't come by what you have or do. You don't have to be anything special to have value. Just being here learning from experience and contributing has value. Everything you learn gives you more ability to contribute on your learning journey. You are so much more than how you look or what you have accumulated. You play many roles and who you are doesn't change. Enjoy the journey, the end is death.

20. **Assertive**. To keep this system in place everyone needs to be assertive. Assertiveness is stronger than aggressiveness and might be interpreted as aggressiveness from someone feeling threatened.

Assertiveness includes tact and kindness along with having a voice. If people don't have a voice and can't speak up, you won't know where you stand with them.

Assertiveness takes training. This is something you can do in your company. Role playing can work to develop this skill. Quiet people are often passive people afraid to speak up. Communicate with them and ask them about their past. If people are passive they might be devious because they are not used to being up front and honest. They will need to get past their fears.

Aggressive people can come off as bullies but they will have more skills. They may challenge you. Instead of putting them down or calling them on their behaviour, have a meeting about the difference between assertiveness vs. aggressiveness. Use examples to show the difference. Get them to step back and forth between passive, aggressive and assertive until they integrate them into being able to hold assertiveness in all situations.

21. **Directness**. Instead of manipulating the synergistic system allows for individuals to be more direct and ask for what they want. People are upfront and honest and feel they deserve when the system permits it. Directness still takes tact and good communication skills. As a leader, be kind with any directness.

22. **Constructive.** This system is focused on everything being constructive. If something isn't constructive, it doesn't belong in this system. Discourage behaviour that is destructive. Communicate the difference. Mutual support, sharing ideas, connecting on goodness, being helpful are all constructive. People who feel whole will take constructive criticism as feedback and adjust behavior.

23. **Centered within self.** Instead of selfish or selfless, people need to be centred within themselves. How they do this is by taking care of themselves first and others second. That includes being considerate of others. If everyone does this, there will be no co-dependency.

24. **Documenting**. Documenting what is necessary is always a good practice. Keeping good records is good business. We live in an X system world so it is always necessary to keep things documented. Enlist everyone's help to keep records documented for the good of all.

25. **Motivation**. Inspiration and encouragement works in a functional system where people have enough skills so they are already doing what they choose. Motivation in this kind of system pulls people forward towards what they want instead of pushing them forward with threats. Curiosity, creativeness, and accomplishment are great motivators. People work here because it is more like play or is a fun workplace and it has purpose and potential. These things increase productivity and performance. Perks that include flexible hours and other flexible benefits, creative challenges, putting trust in employees and employees feeling welcomed and safe are great motivators that create great company cultures.

26. **Inter-dependency**. People work together and are inter-dependent rather than an extreme of either dependent or independent. To be interdependent a person needs to know both dependence and independence to be whole and know the difference. Whole people can share a journey without leaning on each other.

Choice and responsibility rests with each individual person. Let other people experience the emotions that come with their journey. You can only be responsible for how you feel and responsible for your own choices. Don't rescue. Employees who are whole don't need caretaking and working with them is easy.

In personal relationships, relationships based on filling needs are co-dependent. Personal relationship based on filling needs is a trade and is dysfunctional. In business it is different, you get paid by the needs you fill. Business is all about filling needs. Working together to fill the needs of customers interdependently fits a synergistic system.

27. **No Games** played. Head games are not necessary because people feel good and are up front. There are no guilt trips. Responsibility correctly distributed eliminates obligation. Pity is not love and not done.

28. **Shared journey**. In a synergistic group everyone takes responsibility for their part of a shared journey with the organization. It is a choice to be here. We are all sharing a journey and if the journey isn't right, leave. There is no reason to revolt or retaliate because individuals take responsibility for their learning on their own journey as well as for their choice to stay or leave. Sharing the journey is an idea that promotes equality, collaboration and harmony.

29. **Boundaries.** Healthy whole people have natural boundaries. Behaviour is above the line and if someone makes a mistake and realizes they stepped below the line they can step back and re-evaluate. Everyone makes mistakes as they learn. It is good for companies to have discussions about above the line and below the line attitudes and behaviours so there is a common understanding of the issue. It is a kinder way to discuss behaviours that don't work for a positive system.

When people are whole they don't need outside boundaries inflicted on them and they feel freer to be. They have an awareness that goes with live and let live. They know how to manage their own emotions and behaviours. Whole people have real confidence not fake ego confidence.

Freedom, fun, and happiness go together. If the work isn't fun, do something else. If what you are doing doesn't make you happy, it's not right for you. Try something else. Live and let live.

A system built on wanting everyone to enjoy their work will be a synergistic system. People who are having fun do better work and want to stay.

Freedom is a mind-set. Some people don't know how to be free and will not fit in this system. Some people will misuse freedom if given too much. When you observe people you can tell how they feel. Pay attention to your employees. Observe them. Communicate with them. Allow them to share with you so you can understand them, inspire and encourage them.

30. **Respect**. Respect begins with self-respect. If a person doesn't respect themselves they won't respect others. Give respect where due. Give people a chance.

All people deserve respect for having learned what they have from their difficult journey. Everyone has had difficulties in some way. Have compassion.

WORKPLACE COMMUNICATION

USING THE RIGHT WORDS

Eliminate the word "Why." Asking others, "Why did you do that?" sounds judgmental. It is better to ask what or how questions. Can you feel the difference rephrasing the question to, "How did you decide to do that?" instead of why. Would you be more likely to get a constructive answer rather than a reactive answer? Using "what" or "how" gets better information in return from others as well as when you question yourself.

CORRECTING EMPLOYEES

If it is necessary to give constructive feedback or correct anything, say the negative part first, include the word "but" and follow with something good. This is an example. "We can't have your production that slow *but*, I can see that you are being very through and doing good work." The "but" cuts the negative feeling and leaves the person still feeling good about themselves while you still got the first idea across.

MORE ABOUT SYSTEMS

Although there are two seemly opposite systems, it is not about making a judgement that one is bad and the other good or that one is right and the other wrong. Both **operate** systematically creating different results and an organization will constantly move back and forth between the two as it is a dynamic living organism.

Each system requires different thinking and a different style of management. Having more than one option gives leadership a choice. Seeing clearly two opposite systems and comparing them makes obvious what might need to change in a sliding scale between the two. It is the underlying thinking that creates a system and needs to be examined.

One purpose of identifying these two systems is to clarify the problems that people experience working in companies. Sometimes it is difficult to understand why a person is not happy in a company.

It is also useful for an organization to target which kind of system works best for their people or operation. By comparing the two systems one can learn or choose the outcome they want and move in that direction.

Many businesses are built on negativity. Some companies would cease to exist if the system changed. If all people were completely positive many businesses would not be needed. We might not even need the health care we now have.

If everyone had the skills to be positive all the time and wanted to get along, no one would have much to learn. We would only have joy and love. The world would be perfect. We would feel good all the time. All our relationships would be love. There would be no drama. There would be no struggle. There would be abundance for all. There would be no need for lawyers. How many other jobs would go away? What would we watch on TV?

Nothing seems clear when one is dealing with the X System but any negativity is clearly X. Some common behaviors are considered normal but are still X. The eventual outcome of any situation will let you know which system was operating. Unfortunately, sometimes we can only see this looking back. Hindsight is 2020. Each system's outcome is predictable although we can't always know which system we are using in the moment.

What kind of company do you want? Do you want one that employs people that will just do as they are told? If that works for you, consider what would happen if you change. If those same people went to a company that allowed them to think for themselves, they would be waiting for the shoe to drop at any time. They wouldn't know how to manage as they don't know how to manage themselves or their emotions. They are used to following orders. They would be uncomfortable. They don't expect to be happy at work.

Similarly, if you have a company that is authoritarian and threat based, someone who thinks for themselves would not be happy working there. They might create chaos in the system. They might challenge the system as they are not used to watching everything they say. They would question inappropriately for that system. They would upset the hierarchy. They would not be able to be controlled and would feel controlled and uncomfortable. They would not stay.

A mixed system takes extra work to be stable. Some companies have a hierarchy at the top and then hire managers who are more synergistic so that people with more skills will stay. This is hard on the managers as they always have to play a game between the two different systems. It adds stress to their life. The will spend extra time interpreting for each layer in the system.

The X system works a specific way under controlled leadership with rules and imposed boundaries. Lifting control on people without the ability to think and manage themselves, invites chaos until those people learn new skills to get along, see each other as equals, and hold boundaries.

Financial success does not guarantee happiness. Reviewing how a system is operating can predict individual results and the outcome of relationships and groups. A positive system is what we all want to move towards as we evolve in the world.

A system of love would be total freedom and happiness because people would have enough skills, that boundaries don't have to be imposed, and the principle of "doing what works for the highest good of all" would already be in place. It is a process and not an overnight project. So as people take on new ideas their lives change and business changes. *We aren't there yet.*

As people learn new ideas and change their thinking they evolve but sometimes evolve haphazardly. One part of new thinking might not fit with old beliefs and values creating internal conflicts and outside crisis situations. If you change, everyone around you has to change in some degree too.

Similarly, a system like a government or a company, as it moves towards giving people more freedom without those people having the functional skills to make good decisions or the abilities and understanding needed to hold that freedom in place, there will be confusion and problems.

Leadership needs to understand a framework that will lead and educate people into a new system. Integrating a new system requires functional thinking, healthy behaviors, and good emotional skills. Organizational change is an educational process. Most companies are not prepared to do this. Some companies do implement psychological help for employees however; talk therapy is very slow at developing skills. Emotionology coaching is more appropriate because it is fast and is all about developing emotional skills, improving behaviors, and change.

On an individual basis, we are the creator and cause of living in either system. Our individual point of view creates our personal world or our individual learning journey and how we make choices. We can daily create either way – positively or negatively. Natural laws of the Universe operate regardless of which system we use. We can depend on the truth of how either system works.

Some days we see the worst in everything, other days we love everyone. We all move between these two dichotomies and are constantly creating our future as we vacillate back and forth. What do you think is the purpose of this other than for each of us to learn? We each have an individual journey of learning but we also have a larger shared journey. We share a journey with our country and the whole world. This shared journey we participate in is a journey we may feel like we have little control over. Everything in X is limited information and limiting in some way. The feelings that result from the X system are lack, emptiness, inequality, loneliness, fearfulness, struggle, and many other negatives. It doesn't matter how successful you seem to be, "It can be very lonely at the top." Everyone falls off their pedestal.

This book is an educational venue towards positive change in thinking both for individuals as well as organizations. We use these models for workshop participants in their learning journey of becoming an Emotionology Coach. We use the information in these models for individual coaching for people to understand what works for happiness in their lives as well as what works in relationships.

The X system is the way everyone was taught, and every system operated before there was freedom. Now we can reform organizations so that they can have a map for change. A better system would have less turnover and happier people in companies. Understanding both models of thinking, and how they work as systems is a powerful tool by which you can measure other people's behaviors and your own feelings, behaviors, and ideas. You can also measure the health of any organization with this same model. I contend that your individual health is also dependent on how you think positively or negatively.

Our government is X, a hierarchy, set up to reward the highest in the system and control the lowest. It is always a struggle for power. It promotes limited and scarcity thinking. We live in this system and contribute to making a system like this any time we become negative, combative, argumentative, unloving, rebellious, or make comparisons of our self with others to be better than or less than. The synergistic system is not a hierarchy. No one is better than anyone else. Everyone comes from freedom and abundance. Everyone is and feels empowered. This is a goal

Both systems are useful to understand because many people are without skills and people need understanding. When someone is too young to know any better or emotionally limited, one needs to know how to help. Organizations, as a mixed system, can be functional but, be careful to not give mixed signals. Any group as well as any individual will be predominantly slanted towards one system more than the other therefore fitting into one rather than the other.

In theory, anything X will end. Any imaginary success is temporary We all get old, lose our power, and get replaced. The goal is for us to all learn to be positive, enjoy the process, and get along even if it all ends.

As an individual, Donald Trump is a perfect example of a dysfunctional X system thinking, behaviors, and leadership. He is like all the others on the top that don't pay taxes and run the system in their favor as they think they have all the power. But power is always shifting. He will get all the consequences that come with his behaviors. We need a more functional system for government. Let's wait and see what happens with this new dynamic.

Secrets and deception - no governmental official is up front and honest. Don't expect them to be as all X systems serve self-interest. The end justifies the means. Governments always are X system, even if they put out that they are about equality or democracy. They pretend to do good things and really care while governing in fear.

Our government is **co-dependent**, trying to take care of everyone and making people more dependent than independent. Caretaking is really pretended healthy giving—not so. The X system is complicated and convoluted. A system based on love is simplicity.

The history of Russia is interesting in how it played out relative to how systems change. During Peter the Great, Russia was transformed. Although he kept absolute power, which is typical of total Autocracy, he brought stability to the country. His positive vision for his people opened up lucrative Baltic trade routes yet, the system for the people remained backward because the people lacked education. Although Peter was more **positive** than previous rulers, he was ruthless and cruel to keep his people in line. I am sure a more lenient Synergistic system would not have been possible during his time as people were so un-evolved. Any ruler trying to implement a different system would have been considered weak. Changing the system requires education because people need more skills to operate in a different System. Any dysfunction operating within a system will bring the whole X system right back into place.

Under Catherine the Great, there was an opportunity to move to a better system. She instituted some laws of equality and people were becoming enlightened. There was progression towards a slightly better system. The people were given hope for freedom however, there still was no ability to question authority..

The last rulers of the Romanov family promised change, openness and reform, which led the people to think equality and freedom was coming. The ruling class stopped all that and the people rose up to overthrow their government. They had nothing to lose. The people terrorized and killed the Romanov family making it necessary for new leadership to return to strict autocracy to bring back control.

In our present world, what will happen if Trump doesn't follow through with his promises? He said in his speech, "I will give power back to the people; I will not let you down!" How can he fulfill a promise so open to interpretation? Will the public once again revolt? Are we headed towards our own worse situation and less freedom? Have we been trumped?

EMOTION REVOLUTION

We are in an emotion revolution for several reasons. First, as people become more educated and develop their emotional skills they expect more out of life and work. More people are educated today than ever before. Prosperity has lessened the need for struggle and made way for the idea of happiness. Now people feel happiness is possible and they deserve happiness. As a result, they act and respond differently and will put up with less oppression. As any group moves towards increased freedom and abundance, expectations rise.

Second, in the last few generations there has been a change in how society thinks about emotions. The freedom to express emotions has changed. People gained the right to feel and talk about their feelings. This has allowed reactions and drama interfering with smoothness of operations in the work environment. As a result, people want to be heard for their problems and feel entitled to vindication. Many express these emotions from a victim perception.

Third, Society has started co-dependently supporting the underdog and rescuing. The attitudes of victim and entitlement are pervasive and supported. So people get rewarded for their victimhood. The young have grown up coddled and organizations are dealing with entitlement attitudes.

Fourth, the whole country is divided in their political beliefs about religion. Emotions are running high. People fight for their beliefs. Beliefs are individual and often only opinions. Expressing opposing beliefs as truths creates disharmony and conflict. People feel entitled to have and express their beliefs. They don't realize that whatever is true for them might not be true for someone else. Opinions are confused with beliefs.

And, last, the new right to feel and express emotions caused an evolutionary change in the brain. Suppression of emotions by suppressing the images in the mind was common in the old days which gave individuals the skill to step back and be objective. Today many people live in their pictures so their lives become an emotional roll coaster causing loss of control. Feelings emanate from mental images. This makes a person over reactive and less objective. Although, suppressing emotions was an overused skill, this change in the brain is making life difficult. It is an emotional revolution.

According to the documentary " Surviving Progress" (2015) Mentally and physically our brains have changed very little in the past 50,000 years and we have been civilized only in the last 5,000 years. Only our present culture is making a true change from the past. The speed of change has not allowed for us as a society to realize as yet, what really works and what doesn't.

"...culture has taken off at an exponential rate and has really become completely detached from the pace of natural evolution. So we are running 21st -century software, our knowledge, on hardware that hasn't been upgraded for 50,000 years. And this lies at the core of many of our problems. "Quote from documentary "Surviving Progress. "(2015)

SUMMARY OF LIVING IN THE SYNERGISTIC SYSTEM

THE SYNERGISTIC SYSTEM IS A SYSTEM OF FUNCTION.

FEELINGS

Confidence, abundance, self-respect, integrity, courage, safety, helpfulness, ambitiousness, generosity, joy, and all other positive emotions. Feeling OK with self and your journey. Fun and happiness. Faith hope and trust.

PHILOSOPHY

Everyone has a unique individual learning journey and they are all equal. Mistakes are just part of the learning experience. Life is about learning from the adventure of experience and connection. Focus on abundance and happiness and you get more.

SKILLS NEEDED TO KEEP SYSTEM OPERATING

People are pro-active. There is a high degree of self-responsibility. Self-respect and respecting others on their journey. The ability to live and let live. Allowing other people to have their own experience. Self-control and a willingness to learn and grow. Forgiving self and others. Being your own best friend. Seeing and facing reality. Flexible, open and upfront. The ability to be objective and not take things personally. Assertiveness. The ability to stand up for yourself, speak your truth, and question everything tactfully and with good communication. The ability to communicate in a kind understanding way. Thinking for yourself and be able to take feedback. The ability to follow your own intuition. The ability to be centered and considerate. The ability to organize and manage life. Staying in your integrity and being the authentic you. Faith and trust.

MINDSET

Positive attitude true abundance and generosity. Acceptance for where everyone is at this time. Coming from kindness. Collaborative. The intention to connect on goodness.

BEHAVIORS

Compassionate, abundant, kind and considerate communication. Allowing, forgiving, unconditional acceptance of self and others. Keep it simple. Having boundaries. Walk your talk. Trust. kindness, acceptance, truthfulness, helpfulness, openness, letting others have their journey coming from compassion. Accepting that change starts with you. Holding a positive future vision.

BELIEFS AND VALUES THAT KEEP THIS MODEL WORKING

What is right is to do what works for the highest good of all. Believing there is abundance available for everyone. Life is a positive adventure. Experience is valued. Everyone has a unique individual journey all journeys are equal and different. Mistakes equal learning and opportunity. Everyone has equal value as a person. Learning from experience increases your value. Relationships are based on sharing the learning on the journey. True happiness for all is the highest goal. Recognizing that only you can know what is right for you. What is right for you might not be right for someone else. It is important to take care of you before you can take care of others. Knowing your journey is right for you yet it's OK to need to learn something. Sacrifice is unnecessary. Know you are responsible for your own feelings and outcomes. Believing all journeys are equal. High moral values. OK to have fun. Valuing health and happiness. Happiness is more important than being right. Acceptance of others doesn't mean you have to put up with their behaviours if they are unacceptable. It is OK to leave someone. Intimate family deserve your best behaviour. Change and learning is constant.

SYSTEMS

Functional people create a functional system. The thinking of every person in a family or organization affects that group dynamic. Relationships are mutual.

Everyone in the system must do what works for all. It must be an All/Win. Motivation is encourage, inspire, and inform. Information is freely shared. Synergistic Systems have a transparency. People are collaborative - working together for common goals.

www.ingramcontent.com/pod-product-compliance
Lightning Source LLC
Chambersburg PA
CBHW050550280326
41933CB00011B/1786